Division by Zero

Division by Zero

Colin B. Douglas

Waking Lion Press

Copyright © 2016 by Colin B. Douglas. All rights reserved.
Printed in the United States of America.

ISBN 978-1-4341-0406-9

The views expressed in this book are the responsibility of the author and do not necessarily represent the position of the publisher. The reader alone is responsible for the use of any ideas or information provided by this book.

Parts of this book are works of fiction. The characters, places, and incidents in them are the products of the author's imagination or are represented fictitiously. Any resemblance of characters or events to actual persons or events is coincidental.

Published by Waking Lion Press, an imprint of The Editorium

Waking Lion Press™, the Waking Lion Press logo, and The Editorium™ are trademarks of The Editorium, LLC

The Editorium, LLC
West Jordan City, UT 84081-6132
wakinglionpress.com
wakinglion@editorium.com

Contents

Ars Poetica	1
There Is a Young Man	5
"Your Poems Are Querulous"	6
A Parabola Supine on the Floor	7
"Help Me," You Say	8
A Grand Piano on a Pier	9
Sixteen Small Stones	10
Silent Meditations on Torn Lingerie	11
Your Eyes Wide behind Mine	12
Beneath Littered Streets Persist Rumors of Ill Will	13
A Battle Tank Laden with Violets	14
Axels Roll and Clang Down a Desert Highway	15
Let Both Thy Legs Be Spinning Tops	16
Against Black a Torso	17
Suspended in Space	18
Exchanging White Stones Engraved with Our Names	19

Textbook Solutions Always Leak	20
This Rose Unfolding Its Petals	21
Melchizedek and His Bride	22
A Spirit Rises from Our Bed	23
Is Not Babylon a Golden Cup in the Lord's Hand?	24
A Rainbow Straightens; It Is a Flower Stem	25
Rafting to Tahiti	26
You Unlock Yourself	27
Proverbs	28
The Urim of a Jewelry Box	29
Rain Falls through the Night	30
In the Place Where Rain Flies Upward from the Earth	31
Behind a Waterfall an Abandoned Service Station	32
The Hour Is Nigh and the Day Soon at Hand	33
The First Time I Saw Rain through an Edward Hopper Painting	34
The Reason I Stole Shoes from the Legs of an Easel in the MOMA	35

This Is No Accident	36
And God Called the Light Day	37
Speaking of Old Books	38
The Old Woman Who Lives in Deep Woods	39
In the No Thing from Which All Things Rise	40
The Skin of a Telephone Pole	41
The Table Is Set in the Banquet Hall	42
A Flock of Starlings Collapsing Suddenly to a Period	43
Here Is the Secret Exit from the Theater of the Mind	44
A Man in Orange Coveralls and Safety Goggles	45
Sitting in a Camp Chair in a Patch of Alders	46
The Lake's Nipples Quiver under the Gaze of a Receding Paragraph	47
At the Horizon Line of My Woman's Shoulder	48
A Contingent of Undefined Pain Stages an Incident on the Border	49
I Cannot Find Your Kisses on This Map	50
Fleeing the Scene	51

A Salal Leaf Grows from My Palm	52
I Receive a Letter from a Woman Promising Love at an Unspecified Date	54
Your Breasts Are a Bird's Eggs	55
The Woman in the Street Huddles under Her Wings	56
A Period Working Its Way Down the Tube of a Thermometer	57
"Ye Were Also—in the Beginning"	58
Always the First Time?	59
Small Snake Coiled	60
An Eye in Each Fingertip	61
Walking in a Garden We See in the Distance Clocks	62
Arricán France, for a Time	63
Driving a Blue Convertible on a Country Road	64
The Prairie Grass in My Heart	65
In the Grass-Infested Cylinders of a Model T Engine	66
Remorse Is a Decaying House on the Outskirts of Town	67
I Attach Great Importance to Life	68

"No, I Don't Think So"	69
Curl of a Hand	70
Open the Abdomen of the Sun	71
The White Deer That Walks in the Hallway	74
A Breaker Curling Over onto the Shore	75
I Do Not Know Why Deer Wade Up to Their Knees in Blood of Doubt	76
As I Round a Bend in a Canoe a Doe Is Swimming	77
We Should Talk, *Bon Gérard*	78
Tactical Maneuver	79
I Find You at the Box End	81
The Old Woman Who Carries a Basket on Her Back	82
Do You Think God Wants to Withdraw His Ad?	83
God Is That Fat Woman in the Apron	84
As We Sit Together in the Living Room of the Old House	85
Existenz	86
The Sewing Machine Needle of Truth Floats Free	87

SNOWFLAKES DISTANCE THEMSELVES FROM THE PRESIDENT	88
SQUANTO STEPS ON A DRY TWIG	89
STARING DOWN A FISH	90
AFTER THE NEXT WAR	91
BIOGRAPHICAL NOTE	93

Ars Poetica

i

The gift of language presents itself
In a night that lives beneath layers of rock
Words pick their way through slowly
Be patient

ii

Let go of the handful of ropes
The ships full sail will glide away backward
Their destinations written on a motel room wall
Where a man sits alone on the edge of the bed with a clear stone in his hand
Hoping to translate them

iii

Watch for words to rise from a well,
Bright, clear.
Snatch them, one by one.

iv

A burgundy Porsche (it is warm chocolate)
Wraps itself mindlessly around a lamppost
Incites it to flash neon poems.
This occurs with some frequency in the gardens of temples
That hide in the depths of canyons,
In shadows,
Behind boulders,
Beside springs around which deer and lions and many smaller
    creatures
Congregate to consider the meaning of what is etched on the walls.
The woman who walks the canyons
(Sometimes she is old, sometimes she is young;
Sometimes she is naked, sometimes she is clothed)
Sometimes pauses to interpret,
But the animals never think to write her words
(It could be done with a tip of an antler or a claw
And a small offering of blood).
It is rumored that they are written on light
Behind the pages of old books,
And sometimes the pages thin to reveal them.
They may also be enciphered by flashing streetlamps
And the drippings of melting Porsches.

v

Yesterday a stone spoke of dried-up seas and stunted grass
In obedience to rules of prosody laid down by trout that flash in sunlight.
They remember solemnly the girls who dance in woods.
The girls' eyes are large and wide.
They are not fooled by foolish men who lose their shoes when passing through a room,
Who cling by the fingernails to the surface of the smooth sphere that rises from the lake
From beneath the roots of water lilies afloat in the night.
"Forget me not," the night says as it slips behind the moon to rest and heal.
Its wounds gape and are very painful.
It is wounded mysteriously every time it walks in empty streets
Where battle tanks and kelp groves once reigned over a populace of poets and metaphysicians
Who scratched futilely at the faces of tall buildings trying to catch hold.

vi

A raven said:
Unto what shall I liken these mysteries,
    that you may understand?
Behold, who has seen them has seen rain fly up from the earth;
    behold, he has seen it.
Nonetheless, the stones creep beneath the garden,
    forgetful of rain and violets.
The violets peer about expectantly,

but the stones forget to embrace them.
Nonetheless, rain flies up from the earth;
  iron butterflies cavort in sunshine.
Therefore shall the violets remember
  that they have seen fire, have seen rain;
That the river of lies that flows down from that lost star,
  that runs beneath the balconies of a spacious building—
The dreams that stumble into it can remember yet their innocence;
  otherwise, the violets must forsake all hope of marriage.
Behold, may these things not be likened
  unto the sayings of that woman who lives in deep woods,
She who is sometimes old, sometimes young,
  who sometimes goes clothed, sometimes naked?
She sends out dreams to twelve dreamers—
   to one a white rabbit;
   to another an ambassadress of saltpeter;
   to another an iron butterfly;
And so on unto all the twelve,
  unto each in his time,
Unto each according to the word that comes to her
  from the night that lives behind rock.
Each inscribes his dream in the patina of a canyon wall;
  each ponders his inscription;
Each reaches forth to touch the fire that lives behind it,
  behind the rock, behind the night where stones lie with violets.

vii

Touch a word and a whole language trembles in anticipation
And the couple in the cherry tree, lips and tongues

There Is a Young Man

There is a young man, a promising poet, sitting on the edge of a bunk in a civilian internment camp in western Utah, clutching a crystal sphere, and his eyes stop blinking, open. The walls of the barrack are covered with tarpaper, and bare lightbulbs hang from the ceiling on black insulated wiring. The young man is shirtless and his skin is pale. He has just showered (this camp is regularly inspected by the Red Cross and is known for its humane conditions) and his skin smells clean. Someone goes outside to tell a guard, and two internees are ordered to carry the body out and put it in a wheelbarrow and take it to a ditch that has been freshly dug at the edge of the camp just inside the chain link fence and dump it in. It is the first body to go into that ditch. Guards throw dice for the crystal sphere, which is later reported resting on top of the ethyl pump at an abandoned service station in Arizona.

"Your Poems Are Querulous"

"Your poems are querulous."
So says the woman who leaves the table,
Frowning with disapproval.
Querulous? But she may be right,
And I would prefer to hide in a huckleberry bush,
Feet in the roots, hands extended into the leaves

A Parabola Supine on the Floor

A parabola supine on the floor
Imitates cries of sea gulls lost in the sun
Scraps of paper blowing across a desert cry as well but in higher register
The parabola undulates on the swells of the Pacific

"Help Me," You Say

"Help me," you say.
"I can't reach the drawer under my left shoulder blade."
You sit on the edge of a bed,
Flesh glowing in morning light.
I stand on the floor beside you,
Open the drawer,
And see a needle, a thimble, a pigeon feather, a tiny mirror, a
    flowering pear tree,
A slowly moving stream with banks covered by sun-warmed grass,
A miniature oil painting depicting the beheading of a false shaman,
A black seed spat out by Eve.
"I want a pear blossom," you say,
And I pluck one and place it on your left thigh.
Later, emerging from sleep,
I catch a glimpse of a black seed floating away on the stream.

A Grand Piano on a Pier

A grand piano on a pier against a sunset
Plays a fugue slowly
Dice of teeth rattle in a cup
Fall on the pier
In a pattern predicted by equations written in the treble clef
A dwarf in yellow huddled against a piano leg
Picks up the tune in perfect falsetto
The sun after setting shines from his throat

Sixteen Small Stones

Sixteen small stones, white and clear
Sixteen stones engraved with an image of the sun
Sixteen girls with stone eyes guard the door of the temple
Sixteen songs coil about temple pillars
Sixteen dwarves with daffodil feet dance on the sea bottom
Sixteen unicorns twist their horns into insoluble knots
Sixteen ships bombard the custom house of regret
Sixteen fish whirl ecstatically in fire
Sixteen faded memories drip from the ceiling
Sixteen portraits hang beneath a bridge
Sixteen wrecked bridges hold an army at a river
Sixteen lost wars petition for reinstatement
Sixteen brides nail themselves to elevator walls
Sixteen coins mistake themselves for poems
Sixteen islands offer asylum to unsuccessful lies
Sixteen lies wait in darkness for lovers

Silent Meditations on Torn Lingerie

Silent meditations on torn lingerie glisten in summer sun
On wharves of gilt lilies and egg yokes shorn of dogs
Of hairy giraffes burning
Burning on hills of life
In desert
In city
Empty streets melt in glare of mushroom clouds
Let us go down
Let us go down
Let us go down to the sea again
In ships dragged through empty streets
Melting streets
Gutters of pure gold
Sketched on thighs of sad streetwalkers
They have sad eyes
They have red ribbons in their hair
Torn ribbons

Your Eyes Wide behind Mine

Your eyes wide behind mine,
Surprised after long search
Among boulders,
Through canyons,
To come upon such a view.
We somersault backward,
Above tips of fir trees,
Forest beneath us stretching over the horizon.
Rumors pass of an ocean beyond

Beneath Littered Streets Persist Rumors of Ill Will

Beneath littered streets persist rumors of ill will
Toward royal personages who mutter under their breath.
Fourteen varieties of genetically engineered strawberry vines dangle
    from their teeth.
I would be troubled were the sun to splinter against a betrayal,
But meanwhile I take comfort in bark detaching from dead
    aspens—
The fibrous inner tissue makes a wonderful tinder.

A Battle Tank Laden with Violets

A battle tank laden with violets, roots and all, bursts from the pavement,
Hunches its shoulders, on each of which perches a little man
Holding a portrait of Dear Leader.
The curb's eyes look up wide with wonder and fear.
The tank proceeds with self-assurance
Between tall buildings with black façades.
They have many windows with white sills.
Ghosts of dreams of memories of courage rush about hysterically,
Mindless of the futility of hopes to escape
Into the depths of a lake among stems of water lilies.
Better to hide behind a portrait of Dear Leader.
The tank moves on past the edge of the city, to the beach, toward the sea.
It disintegrates into sand.

Axels Roll and Clang Down a Desert Highway

Axels roll and clang down a desert highway,
Trade amongst themselves stories of loves lost in canyons of desire,
Where the drivers of dairy trucks shave their legs before prayer
And remember ancient days
When a beam of sunlight reflected from a rabbit skull
Could find sanctuary in a forgotten book.
These stories slip from a lover's fingertips
And inscribe themselves in blue ink on the skin of a beloved,
On the skin along the spine.

Let Both Thy Legs Be Spinning Tops

Let both thy legs be spinning tops.
A window pane that cuts us in half
Would find more satisfaction in cotton threads
Hung from a clothesline across the abyss of desire.
The sides are sandstone cliffs red in noonday sun.
White rabbits browse in the crevices.
At the bottom of the canyon a caravan of Buicks,
Glass flashing, roofs hot,
Picks its way carefully among boulders.
We park at the canyon's edge,
The road narrowing, turning downward
Under pine trees, blocked by boulders.
We see through the windshield over the edge
The caravan of Buicks picking its way.
Both thy legs are spinning tops.

Against Black a Torso

Against black a torso
Beside it a cluster of crystals
Grasp the crystals
Edges and points
Clear, sapphire
In the depth of crystal your eyes
Open, unblinking

Suspended in Space

Suspended in space
Spread-eagled face to face
Our hands nailed
Our feet nailed
Our breath mingled
The suns in our loins fused

Exchanging White Stones Engraved with Our Names

Exchanging white stones engraved with our names,
We join the procession into the sun.

Textbook Solutions Always Leak

Textbook solutions always leak:
Sand in a child's pail finds its way to the sea;
The vertex of a parabola opens to a troupe of clowns.
These are consequences of an oft-ignored axiom:
Pharà ba ten ma na tian,
Malikna ba ten sa ánia.

This Rose Unfolding Its Petals

This rose unfolding its petals
Must be enjoyed discreetly
To avoid inciting insurrection
Among software designers in white shirts
Who wait at train stations in the early hours of desire
When the Word flows down the faces of tall buildings like
    dripping paint,
For the alternative surely is chaos:
Brass bands and clowns invading Sunday meetings
As conducting officers throw up their hands to declare,
"I surrender to joy!"
As newly-weds explore the *Kama Sutra* in temple gardens.

Melchizedek and His Bride

Melchizedek and his bride roll with abandon in grass.
Words once lost swarm from every blade.

A Spirit Rises from Our Bed

A spirit rises from our bed,
Withholds its hand,
Its head a seer stone:
See the flower garden
Bright in sunlight.
You offer an azalea,
A snap dragon, a tiger lily.
We stand on a bridge that disintegrates,
A cloud of butterflies.
We fly with them.

Is Not Babylon a Golden Cup in the Lord's Hand?

Is not Babylon a golden cup in the Lord's hand?
It collects light;
A woman dances in it;
Veils whirl about her,
Brush the waxed finish of a new automobile,
Red and gleaming,
All in harmony with the owner's manual for the universe
Kept secure in a box
At the center of the Crab Nebula,
Or if not there, surely elsewhere—
No one has ever doubted it.

A Rainbow Straightens; It Is a Flower Stem

A rainbow straightens; it is a flower stem.
Be careful—the box in which it is stored
Is a treacherous cat that has walked on the water of desire
That puddles seductively on the settee in the operating room
Where children examine through crystalizing eyes
A book illustrated with colored plates
Of the atrocities committed in Nanking.
They are explicit as a handful of rabbits' teeth on an unmade bed.
The rainbow knows but is secure in its box,
Observing dispassionately through a bedroom window
The maneuvers on a hillside of a squadron of toy automobiles
Training for the next war.
It will begin in August (not this August)
And flow down the ravine, down from the hill,
A river of tiny wheels and crystalized eyes.

Rafting to Tahiti

Daneel Olivaw and André Breton are rafting to Tahiti.
They invite Enoch,
Who is detained by a late vision
But promises to join them for a game of gō
And lends them a seer stone found in a nest of Easter eggs,
Pastel blue and yellow,
Like these flowers floating about our bedroom.
They orbit around the clock, a wind-up.
The yellow ones talk with the seer stone in anxious whispers.
It says there could be lunch with Gauguin,
But he is annoyed by false ticks of the clock.
They are dried kisses dropping one per second onto his wet canvases.
The clock itself sits ignored on a corner of the raft.
Raindrops blue and yellow freckle the face of that brown girl who counts them.
They are the true ticks of the clock.
Poets know this,
And brown girls
Whose breasts project wiring diagrams onto the walls of Gauguin's hut.

You Unlock Yourself

You unlock yourself
And swing back the door between your ribs and your navel
To allow the golden wire coils of a symphony of insurrection
To spill forth across both sides of the bed onto the floor
Through the door into the kitchen to liquefy
It is water two inches deep
I attempt to squeegee it together
To hold it against a wall away from the stove
Where a large kettle of broth is coming to a boil
Light reflected from the coils flashing on the walls and ceiling
For an instant we are a full-grown cherry tree heavy with fruit bursting from the ground
I help you collect the coils in handfuls and stuff them back into the darkness
And you push me inside and close the door and lock it

Proverbs

The swift polarity of prying eyes like sin waiting at the door
Eats cherries through the wanton nights of used car lots under
  duress.
A hand beneath a blouse seeks trails through constellations of
  doubt
That rotate on ordinates of intercalated wantonness.
The ionized kisses of a mistress of antiquated wars are not more
  beautiful
Than a bouquet of doubts on a windowsill on the morning of an
  execution.
A windowsill undulating between two colors of a rainbow
Is the analog of hammer blows in the interstices of a rattlesnake's
  vertebrae.
The undulations of the Andromeda Galaxy are sweet as a
  rattlesnake's eyes,
But the loves of used car lots pierce like an antiquated war's tooth.

The Urim of a Jewelry Box

The urim of a jewelry box whispers endearments to the thummim
   of a suspension bridge in the throes of temporary
   dismemberment,
As hanging in air over a rising river of piano notes in high register
   they wonder together at five things:
The way of a lark's tongue with seven-cornered dice,
A promising kiss from Sacagawea contorting in a secret
   compartment of Meriwether Lewis's spy glass,
A flash of cannon fire held in secret and reluctant reserve from the
   Mexican War,
A way of looking at a blackbird dismissed by establishment critics
   as the final belated cowardice of a maimed gun-runner
But recognized by frequenters of reptile zoos on Route 66 as a
   stroke of pure intelligence from beyond the night where stones
   and violets exchange caresses.
Then beyond the penultimate ridge a final crescendo of piano
   notes tumbling up the face of a heaving talus slide of cartridges
   full metal jacket specially engineered for full automatic fire
And finding in the press of one more key apotheosis in a backward
   somersault by the jewelry box and the suspension bridge into
   the violet-colored stars at the center of the galaxy

Rain Falls through the Night

Rain falls through the night,
Sleep hiding,
Maybe under the stage where the sins of my youth prance and leer.
When it returns, we will lie side by side and talk
Of the time when I and the girl were naked and I was a boy,
When we talked with the rabbits and the deer,
Before she began to talk with the snake.

In the Place Where Rain Flies Upward from the Earth

In the place where rain flies upward from the earth,
Girls weave grass and random threads of night.
They make baskets for the collection of buttons
That spring in full blossom from idle conversation;
Girls who stand half revealed in doorways of long halls.
They beckon with hands of four fingers.
They live in glass houses of lavender tint;
Equations etched on the walls trail over the windowsills.
The nipples of the equations gaze brazenly out from between
    parentheses.
The aureoles are in watercolor.
To make baskets with four-fingered hands is a rare talent.
The patterns woven into the baskets are revealed by shamanic hares
Who share the girls' beds through long nights of computation.
The resultant equations trail over the windowsills,
Enlace themselves in patterns of equivocal time spread across the
    grounds,
Down to the edge of the great lake on which a white house has
    been built not far from shore.
Its windows are lavender.
Through a lower window a girl looks out, offering a bouquet of
    buttons.
She speaks equations.
Her lips move unheard from this distance.

Behind a Waterfall an Abandoned Service Station

Behind a waterfall an abandoned service station decays under
  Arizona sun
On Route 66 of an old man's desire
As the pages of a Louis L'Amour paperback turn yellow and brittle.
Read it while sitting on a rock beside the highway—
The robot army that flows over a distant ridge
Will divide and pass harmlessly on both sides around you
(The robot soldiers dream of sleep on beds of dew-damp violets).
You can read this promise in a note hidden in a coffee can by Jubal
  Sackett.
It was guarded faithfully for years by a girl in a light summer dress
Whose brain lies in precisely divided sections on the service station
  counter.
She hid the note in a concrete wigwam until the wigwam was
  commandeered by a robot officer
During the war with a cousin of Gadianton who threatened the
  visible desert
With a visible flood of visible treacherous memories of a kiss,
Before the girl's brain surrendered to inevitable dissection near the
  ethyl pump.
(If this is cryptic, look for the solution stored in glyphs in the
  fragments of a broken crystal sphere.)
In the run-up to the war, she served as a spy for the robot army,
Was known for her magical tongue that had licked every line of
  every glyph,
Encoding it with the coordinates of every waterfall behind which
  old men hide.

The Hour Is Nigh and the Day Soon at Hand

The hour is nigh and the day soon at hand
When the ambassador of the moon's blood
Turns the key to open that museum
Where the heads of the apostate kings are displayed.
It will be on a clear glass night freshly blown,
When the sun's hearse arrives early at the concert hall.
That is the first sign. The second sign
Is the sudden evaporation of the official musicians
Under the very eyes of a visiting trumpeter,
The one who leads the little dog
By a leash of false prophecies.
The musicians think themselves clever to disguise themselves
In the clothes made of the trumpeter's nose hairs,
Or so it has been thought by soldiers whose eyes
Falling from their sockets roll and rattle
Together down the streets where a cheering crowd
Has gathered all night for a victory parade.
"And I will burn them up," saith the ambassador,
"In a bonfire of self-recognition."

The First Time I Saw Rain through an Edward Hopper Painting

The first time I saw rain through an Edward Hopper painting was a Christmas when the two sparrows of my greatest regret were dragged down the highway by a moving van driven by the last shot fired in the war between the sphinxes. Their bones protrude from the sand like Japanese fans planted in the desert of our discontent. Few of us are content with the fruit that derives from that dynamite forest, our legs protruding from under the bed serving as question marks on a billboard of desire that paints your forehead with tiny figures of Gandy dancers in slow motion. (None of this has ever found its way into a Hopper painting.)

The Reason I Stole Shoes from the Legs of an Easel in the MOMA

The reason I stole shoes from the legs of an easel in the MOMA was that rain was crawling across the floor with four dog hairs in its teeth. I had never done that before, except in the case of extreme degradation by pots of boiling broth distributed to vagrant mannequins in the last workshop of radiant hypocrisy. My guilt is an Egyptian barge carrying poems and the raisins preferred by dogs underneath the Nile all the way to the split infinitives at the top of the dial. This is not to be explained to children whose eyes form the center line of a highway.

This Is No Accident

This is no accident.
Its roots extend past that Kuiper Belt of consciousness
Where on the shaded porch of an overlooked house
Three abstract daughters of a half-conjugated verb
Leap from an airship of obsolete wars.
This is according to a musical score delivered by a rabbit on the eve
  of love,
When gravel flung across a highway agitates for change.
Let us be less dismissive of reports from the front
Transmitted telepathically by rows of sparrows
Sitting on telephone lines.
Their minds are green
But good for carrying groceries
Across miles and miles of barren waste.
This is the wish of the three daughters.
They lay themselves down on a strip of aluminum siding
Feet to head, feet to head.
They meditate on transcriptions of sleeping stories
Whispered from the upper thigh of one of them,
Though she is shy to admit it.

And God Called the Light Day

And God called the light Day,
And the darkness he called Night.
So very simple,
More so than the radiance of boats that leave their slippers by the fireside
When they glimmer away,
Moths bedazzled by visions of deer in great troupes
That scratch at the brick fronts of dissolving buildings hoping for remission
Of the residual guilt of grass in the twilight of a kiss.
The grass parts before our liquid steps
As a ray of pure intelligence from Alpha Centauri Bb
(Though its existence is questioned)
Is refracted through a dewdrop
That divides itself by zero.

Speaking of Old Books

Speaking of old books,
There is one on the third shelf down,
Third from the left,
On the Showman's Trail,
A secret compartment cut into the pages.
It holds a cedar-wood box.
In the box is the palace
Of the Little Lame Prince.
At the highest level of the southwestern tower
Is a room where a fire is kept,
Though the room is rarely visited.
Under a vase on a small black table,
In an envelope sealed with red wax,
Is a Christmas card
Depicting a sleigh ride,
A village steeple,
Silver glitterdust for falling snow,
As I am clasped by your legs
In zero gravity

The Old Woman Who Lives in Deep Woods

The old woman who lives in deep woods
Is aware of developments in the capital,
For news travels fast through the root systems,
A fact often overlooked in the histories
That generations of urban spiders have woven into their webs;
But her eyes are the dewdrops on the filaments.

In the No Thing from Which All Things Rise

In the No Thing from which all things rise,
Trees, when they make love,
Conjugate the orbit of the square root of a thigh.

The Skin of a Telephone Pole

The skin of a telephone pole has the texture of cardboard boxes out of tune,
Each one sounding the alarm to warn the birds who say no,
The big ones that hang from a chain stretched between towns,
In one of which survives a small independent movie theater
Where school children pry out their teeth with scissors,
Leaving each pair when they are finished impaled upright on the top of a fencepost,
A fence across southwest Oregon to keep out itinerant dreams
Of a woman who offers a mango seed
Flat in her palm as a piano keyboard stretching to the horizon.
"The car won't start," the woman says.
It is parked on the shoulder of a road in the country where worn-out love is stacked like tires behind service stations.
Then climbing in the superstructure of a bridge made of balsa wood sticks,
Carefully guarding a clear stone in my pocket,
I remember that I am already late for morning formation.
There will be a court martial.
I will present as my defense the black keys of the mango seed,
But I know that the defense of Oregon is already fatally compromised,
And I regret this as the eye of a needle regrets the passage of escaping motor oil.

The Table Is Set in the Banquet Hall

The table is set in the banquet hall:
White napkins, crystal, and flowers;
At each place a fading photograph of a war bride.
The walls are red and hung with oil paintings.
At the end of the hall a child plays on the floor,
A girl in a white dress.
A net of quivering language drops from the ceiling
But remains hovering above her.
The sound of one piano note could release it.

A Flock of Starlings Collapsing Suddenly to a Period

A flock of starlings collapsing suddenly to a period suspended
　　against the sky
Is reminiscent of the membrane that connects the whisperings of
　　lovers to the engines of eighteen-wheel trucks
That speed through the mirror-walled labyrinth called history
The black point marks the boundary between the memory of a first
　　kiss followed by a first laying of bare hands on a bare back
And the meditations of mannequins abandoned on a beach
One of them, suspicious of the others, concentrates on the image
　　of a snake coiled in sunshine on a compost heap
When you approach them they all assume the aspect of new
　　flowers in a garden of suspect conjugations
You yourself can escape suspicion by concentrating on
meadows,
rabbits,
red-tiled rooves,
thin-gloved hands,
leaps of logic,
leaping salmon,
centipedes,
mice,
empty soup cans,
tunnels of abandoned uranium mines in southern Utah,
the vanishing of a river into sand,
any horn of any of Daniel's beasts,
the typography of the text that veils the face of one that you have
　　loved

Here Is the Secret Exit from the Theater of the Mind

Here is the secret exit from the theater of the mind that floats on a black river
Sometimes it stands in glaring sunlight on the red earth of a street in a Brazilian village
The theater, that is
It is the last refuge of young brides who emerge in pairs from the splitting bark of pine trees
If you lie for several hours supine on the street in the later afternoon with your eyes fixed on the equations unfurling in the upper atmosphere
The girl in the ticket booth will come and lift you by the hand
And give you answer to your prayers concerning the source and the destination of the black river
Where it empties into the warm sea of flowers and memories red with old hesitation
The interior of the theater is cool and dark
The box seats are especially well positioned for viewing assassinations in real time

A Man in Orange Coveralls and Safety Goggles

A man in orange coveralls and safety goggles climbing carefully down a ladder inside an enormous concrete vat of boiling water lets go of the ladder and without a sound or motion signifying alarm or pain slips into the water and floats face up. After the body is recovered in a complex and lengthy operation involving chains and grappling hooks it is determined by a forensic team flown in by the FBI at the request of the local police chief that the man probably is dead before he hits the water. A few days later it is reported by a local television station that the chief has for several years carried on an affair with the man's wife, who since early adolescence has been obsessed by a secret fetish for having the backs of her thighs caressed with fresh flowers. There is no evidence, however, of any complicity by either the chief or the wife in the man's death, and no charges are ever brought against them. Curiously, the media never address the question, what is the purpose of the vat of boiling water? And that despite the fact that runoff from the vat has for years irrigated lush and brilliant fields of tulips on the rooftops of Los Angeles office buildings. When the wife is asked about this use of the water as she is interviewed by a reporter while walking naked through a tunnel of mirrors beneath the city, dragging her finger tips lightly along the surface of the glass, she refers the reporter to the appendix of an exhaustive report on the cultivation of tulips, the only known copy of which is classified "Top Secret—POTUS Eyes Only" (everyone involved in its preparation having been subjected to a memory wipe) and kept in a vault in the Oval Office with a blue dress. The case then disappears entirely from the news.

Sitting in a Camp Chair in a Patch of Alders

Sitting in a camp chair in a patch of alders trying to ignore the eyes that watch from a leaf
Seeds pour steadily from a rift in the sky
Each has an eye
The situation is alarming
And the clock on the tower of the municipal building adjacent to the alder patch speaks in tongues
For those who can interpret, it reports without judgment the loves of seafarers from the next county
Or the next century
The solution to the puzzle is written on the sails of small ships rotting with skepticism

The Lake's Nipples Quiver under the Gaze of a Receding Paragraph

The lake's nipples quiver under the gaze of a receding paragraph
The embarrassment of the trees is palpable
The sun bleeds out on a carpet of desire
Paper cups will scoop up the residue
And spread it on a table built of fresh disappointment
Look for the map drawn on the surface of the lake
Touch it—it vibrates
Its continents are mist sucked back into a bottle
Its mountains are the eyes of a feral cat
Surprised in the act of love with a bunch of crabgrass
Its oceans are named *in absentia*
Its meridians are snipped by scissors
The scissor blades that are long-stemmed flowers
That kneel on the map table of prayer

At the Horizon Line of My Woman's Shoulder

At the horizon line of my woman's shoulder
A tank regiment pauses to reconnoiter.
The tanks are very small
But as dangerous as wire threaded from the tip of a snake's tail to the tips of its tongue.
I pick my way toward my woman through webs of tripwires.
They reflect the light of half-memories
Of a red button at rest on the tip of my tongue,
Of flowers picked in the garden where the teardrops of a forgotten war hide from the spies of the morning,
Where the prisoners that survive vivisection in the interrogation tents of hope lie in wait,
Hidden in discarded seed packages
In the garden where memory is a pair of scissors that snips a battle plan at its root.

A Contingent of Undefined Pain Stages an Incident on the Border

A contingent of undefined pain stages an incident on the border between sorrow and an alarm clock.

This is an attempt to provoke a war, but if hostilities break out you can hide behind any numeral of the clock.

You will notice that the clock is growing feathers—you may pluck it bare as time's thigh tattooed with a map out of this hotel where disaffected syntax watches from inside the bed posts.

It is prudent, however, not to notice that time darts through the hallway and around the corner to hide from the sheriff with grotesquely thick legs who searches for it here every night.

Avoid touching his legs—beneath his trousers they are bundles of feathers with many mouths that will attempt to suck you in to the holding tank of the clock's unclaimed ticks.

Eventually the night clerk, who is a woman of a certain age, will come around with the number of the feathers.

It is said to be the security code for the lock on the exit door, if you understand the dialect in which she speaks it.

If you attempt to copulate with her, you will find that she wears always one more layer of clothing.

I Cannot Find Your Kisses on This Map

I cannot find your kisses on this map
And the roof is made of flower stems
It will not last the night
Of rain so bright it cannot be described mathematically
Other lovers quarrel in the street
Their clothes hang from the arch of a bridge
Against a backdrop of complex plumbing
From which starlings flow upward
I would hold your shoulders and kiss you while hiding among the starlings
But I cannot find your kisses on this map

Fleeing the Scene

FLEEING THE SCENE
FLEEING RESPONSIBILITY
FLEEING THE INTERVIEW
There is a good deal of fleeing, a young woman points out,
One who is skilled at vaginal contraction.
Eve learned of that skill from the white hare that prayed through the spider's web.
It spoke with her at length as the waters receded gradually toward the edges of the earth.
These thoughts revolve with the planets as one passes through the city square.
These buildings—they will wash away when the floods return.
The secrets that hide in them fork on an endless decision tree.
One thinks of settling comfortably into the driver's seat of a red convertible
And driving leisurely through southern California,
Through the stratified fissure that opens in Ginsberg's best lines,
Sandstone orange, sandstone red, sandstone black,
Smelling hot in the sunlight.
It leads to a beach, where, standing in the sand in highly polished shoes,
One remembers the smell of a freshly washed and ironed blue dress
That descends over a young woman's freshly washed body
As gently, as quietly, as smoothly as a robin's egg descends into the gullet of a snake.

A Salal Leaf Grows from My Palm

A salal leaf grows from my palm
It does not compute interest
As a canoe emerges from the leaf
Looks about
Sees that traffic is heavy on the freeway
Going softly
It parts the salal bushes on the median strip
Going softly
Salal growing on the stairs
A dust cloud pervades the imagination
Fishhooks dangled in the ivy
And why must I wait so long for a kiss from the woman who lives
   in the woodshed?
She smiles from a block of wood
A river slips silently and unobtrusively from beneath the woodpile
Creeps under the door and bolts for the sea
Carrying her smile in its pocket
The smile is very knowing
It has lived where the songs emerge whole from loaves of bread
What its fingers have touched is the first secret that lives beneath
   the stairs
The salal bushes are deeply rooted in it
The canoe sits high on the water
A quantum of salal leaves is very light
A quantum of reminiscence flits in and out of existence
Now it sits on the prow of the canoe
Now it slides down the arm
The smile is very knowing

The balustrade creeps down the slope toward the river
White, it fails to attain its objective
The further end lies in fragments
The fingers have touched them
The fingers know that the hand cannot grasp itself
The quantum of reminiscence progresses along the sleeve

I Receive a Letter from a Woman Promising Love at an Unspecified Date

I receive a letter from a woman promising love at an unspecified date.
It evokes a constellation of memories—
The warm water of the river that flows from beneath a small house just outside the edge of a pine forest;
A fold of silk;
A heap of rose petals in my cupped right hand,
In each an eye that has seen the dawn
Where songs hide curled like four-week fetuses in the corners beneath stairways.
The late president clutches with bloody hands at the stiletto in the base of his throat.
I am nearly overcome by drowsiness as I read.
Her name is Legion, and the edges of her shadow are feathered.
Resolving to ignore the drowsiness, I walk out into the street,
Which as I walk becomes a canyon of Wingate sandstone
Where water is scarce but can be found trickling from faucets at approximately shoulder height.
I recognize the contours of her belly in the sandstone adjacent to one of the faucets
And take refuge from the sun by sitting in the shade within her navel.
Her letter is tattooed on my back.

Your Breasts Are a Bird's Eggs

Your breasts are a bird's eggs, smooth but not speckled
Sleeping curled on your left aureole
I dream of the afternoon when we are glyphs etched in desert patina
The sun is high but we are on the southern wall of a canyon and the sun never touches us
After your breasts hatch I will keep the broken shells in a basket woven of your eyelashes

The Woman in the Street Huddles under Her Wings

The woman in the street huddles under her wings
She is ignored by passers-by, who are preoccupied by the moths that flutter in the hollows of their silhouettes
She grieves for the legless children who hide behind the false building fronts that have been set up along the street by anonymous volunteers for the benefit of tourists
The tourist industry in this country predates by many years the publication of Boileau's *Art Poétique*
But be careful of the ants—they have friends in high places where the historical archives are burned for heat in winter
Winter comes unexpectedly in this country close behind the elk herds that step hesitantly out from between the false fronts like rancid guilt
When I was a legless child hiding behind a false front I sometimes looked up from scriptural texts to see the herds step out from beyond the horizon

A Period Working Its Way Down the Tube of a Thermometer

A period working its way down the tube of a thermometer pauses for conversation with the birds of late desire
I have no idea where it has laid the axel discarded by the moving van of regret
I pat its down-covered belly with an ivory drumstick
It purrs like a cat whose legs are borrowed from a dinner table
Stare at the period long enough and all six of its wings unfurl into a winter of harpsichord notes

"Ye Were Also—in the Beginning"

"Ye were also—in the beginning"
The words excreted in the sap of an alder tree
I lay myself under it to sleep and dream
Of secure employment as an implementation software designer
And wake to the reality of a river of elk antlers
Flowing from beneath the roots

Always the First Time?

Always the first time?
A handful of grapes
The little fox whose teeth are box cutters
Leads the procession out from the shade and the cool of the
	mission church
Into the bright sunlight of apocryphal polemics
A soap dish could demolish the argument
Always the first time
I place a peeled grape between your teeth

SMALL SNAKE COILED

Small snake coiled
In drawer of dressing table
Built of red cedar
(Fragrant)
In corner of lady's private chamber
She is the one whose head is a glittering fountain
Or a sedge of bitterns
(It is said to depend on the position of Saturn relative to Orion)
She was one's lover once
Before the stream that issues from beneath the cottage
Divided into four and evaporated
Into glittering confetti
Reflecting a face on every flake
It is familiar
It was once the lady's

An Eye in Each Fingertip

An eye in each fingertip
Lingering doubts about the efficacy of certain prayers
Looking out from the center of a crystal sphere
The stairway festooned with yellow flowers
A brief kiss on lips
A walk in a garden
The eyes of your fingertips blink rapidly

Walking in a Garden We See in the Distance Clocks

Walking in a garden we see in the distance clocks hanging in the arches of a bridge
Your white hand rests palm up
We have made love under that bridge
The memory of it is a cloud of dragonflies rising up from the hand

Arricán France, for a Time

Arricán France, for a time
Splitting a mullein fruit with a thumbnail
At the moment when pleasure is incandescent pain
A heavy serpent descends between hills
Scales glisten in the sunlight
Arricán is the word that fills its mind
See its eye that is a clock
From where do such words come?
A mullein fruit holds many seeds
Incandescence is a swan that opens its breast with two hands

Driving a Blue Convertible on a Country Road

Driving a blue convertible on a country road in sunshine, this girl's head resting on my shoulder, her head white and shaped like something made of rubber, but her breasts firm and gleaming in the sunlight, her dress with a floral pattern (the front of the dress being cut away to expose her chest and upper abdomen) smells freshly washed and ironed. Then we are climbing together in the cables of a suspension bridge, the cables also gleaming in the sunlight. From this vantage we look on busy streets painted with unknown letters, but we recognize the word. Will she go away if I attempt to kiss her? But the rubber thing that is her head has no lips.

The Prairie Grass in My Heart

The prairie grass in my heart is silent as a broken pane of glass
And sleep remains elusive: it spills from my hands dry and
    crumbling

In the Grass-Infested Cylinders of a Model T Engine

Intimation of regret in the grass-infested cylinders of a Model T
  engine set on sawhorses under walnut trees
The grass dry as the memory of virginity in a cluttered warehouse
  of remorse
The oil pooled on the ground of being looks about warily
Beware the rainbow sheen it is a map
And the warehouse is marked in blue
And is not trustworthy

Remorse Is a Decaying House on the Outskirts of Town

Remorse is a decaying house on the outskirts of town
Beyond are fields where the grass is uncut and dry
The woman who looks out the window has binoculars
She is a magpie
She is the fragrance of a hand of playing cards jack of diamonds
Her thoughts are a curve in a stairway
Her thoughts are the curve of an elliptical seerstone
We loved her once
Wind sways the grass
The flight of a magpie persists

I Attach Great Importance to Life

I attach great importance to life
Standing here on this threshold of
The door that opens in two directions
Standing here on the edge of
A watermelon seed
On a sunlit street on a strip of beach
Girls in bathing suits water droplets on their skin refracting sunlight
Where it makes perfect sense to say that ninety percent of the instances of HIV occurring in the shells of pigeons' eggs are attributable to the absence of orange Kool-Aid in the pudenda of boxcars, the ones that have painted on their outer surfaces the remnants of alphabets lost for centuries as Sherpa guides meditate on the peels of oranges apples bananas all manner of goat and numerous species of vascular plant
Where a word turns on its axis
Where a word's color becomes another

"No, I Don't Think So"

"No, I don't think so."
"But why, if the corner of the door is curling like the corner of a sheet of white paper?"
"That's just what they said. The smoke curls above the roofs."
"Then it won't be today."
But it is the smoke, after all
As we stroll on the beach
The buttons under our feet so deep and slippery
This mixture of invective and possibility appears on a terrorist watch list
It spills, black sand, off both sides of my palm

Curl of a Hand

Curl of a hand
Curl of a leaf
Curl of a petal
Curve of a feather
The feather lies on the highway
It is regulated by an agency that lives under the skin of the head
Fishhooks attach themselves to the head
Their leaders radiate outward by static electricity
The petal is the skirt of an emaciated girl
She is a forgotten daughter of a Fisher King
Who wraps his limbs around the trunk of a pine tree
As tall as the ceiling of a drunkard's kitchen
I sleep with a petal over each eye
They are translucent and very suggestive

Open the Abdomen of the Sun

Open the abdomen of the sun
Its entrails spill onto the beach
The fish heads of ignominy are painted on the walls—blue streaks
We should leave in the morning—there will be anger under the stairs
I think the crack in the window glass is an *ad hominem* argument
And the cracks in the pavement have gone fishing with a flock of sparrows
I sit on the edge of a bed with my eyes closed
My eyes are closed and my shoulders sag forward
My eyes are closed and my hands dangle between my knees
I smell smoke
I smell a buffalo
I smell a rattlesnake
I smell the skin of my woman
She has washed in the river, which is far away
My old woman died
The rattlesnake grows large under the floor of my shack
The buffalo are gone and no one knows where
I smell smoke
The walls of my house are rubber sheets
They quiver when they are touched
The aspen trees outside
Their branches reach upward white
If they could get jobs in the city they would send money to their wives
But they wrap themselves in rubber sheets and dream

But there is no cause for alarm just because white rabbits twist
    their necks into question marks
This happens every day in the rubber houses where gangs of heroin
    traffickers squat against the walls practicing self-pollution
And in the morning we shall go down to the sea
Where the long black ships wait
We shall lead the white rabbits by leashes
We shall answer all their questions
Meanwhile Odysseus waits on the beach
On a driftwood log before a fire
The neon cables blue red yellow intense white
Snake forth from the gate of Ilium into the water on both sides of
    him
What was it all for? he wonders
The signs of the musical notes rising up from the beach are black
    and ephemeral
They are mysterious as the stones
He is not Odysseus
He must be called something
He shall be called Enoch
The palm of his hand strokes the irregular edge of the galaxy
And that is just the beginning
When the procession of girls in white gowns approaches in the
    distance
They are an uncountable throng
Their inner thighs rub distractingly together as they walk one inch
    above the stones of the beach
He collapses inward into himself
The further in he goes the bigger he gets
The girl who leads the procession holds a crystal sphere on her
    open hands

He is the sphere
And this is the reason why a rubber band hooked on a nail and stretched to the breaking point
Considers itself fortunate if it finds itself walking with white rabbits into the center of an argument
That is a spider's web glistening with rain and looking through itself into the distance along the beach
At Enoch and Odysseus waiting together on a driftwood log for the procession to arrive
Each girl bearing a lamp
Except the first, who bears the crystal sphere
That in reality is the galaxy the irregular edge of which Enoch strokes with the palm of his hand absent-mindedly
Confident that love will find him

The White Deer That Walks in the Hallway

The white deer that walks in the hallway,
   the deer that was seen by lost children,
its hooves are embroidered with patterns of usury;
   they are memorials of a previous regime.
One remembers this while motorcycling on the causeway
   between hope and the image of white on a wall,
   or the thumbprint of evil and the portrait of an embroideress.
It is so difficult to distinguish the threads from the fabric;
   and your arms brush the dew from the branches of a cedar
   as you walk in a hallway that forever narrows,
or the sunlight from the walls; it is paint flaking,
   as in the prophecies etched on the deer's antlers.

A Breaker Curling Over onto the Shore

A breaker curling over onto the shore
I turn to you
Your breath in my nostrils
The smell of you in my hair
I cannot distinguish my skin from yours
Hand in hand we walk through a wall
We levitate
We pass through archways
The sea always beneath us
The sea surging through the archways beneath us
The sea in our loins and surging
We stand by a wall
The wall transparent
Beyond it always the sea

I Do Not Know Why Deer Wade Up to Their Knees in Blood of Doubt

I do not know why deer wade up to their knees in blood of doubt;
   this is the mystery of grace and the tenderness of a rose petal.
A rumor of it passes through the crowds on the street
   like a warm breeze of heresy through cracks in the window
      panes of the chancellery
   as sticks rattle along the cobblestones.
There is the doorway;
   it leads to the men's room all white porcelain and terraced.
It is difficult to distinguish the urinals from the wash basins;
   one does not want to err on that score;
and the lights are on late in the chancellery,
   it being likely that an attack is planned for the early hours of the
      morning.
A rumor of it passes through the crowds.
The generals are perched in a row with legs dangling over the
   upper terrace of the men's room;
they are decidedly opposed to sodomy
   and are vigilant to prevent it,
and they observe closely the patrons
   who are anxious to protect their shoes from the water that
      overflows the trough at the bottom of the wall,
but that is impossible,
   and they are uncertain about the blood;
it possibly is menstrual,
   though the deer seem unconcerned.

As I Round a Bend in a Canoe a Doe Is Swimming

As I round a bend in a canoe a doe is swimming across through the warm brown water.
She sees me and turns back and scrambles up the muddy bank and vanishes into the tamarisk.
Beyond the tamarisk at the bottom of a sandstone cliff are glyphs.
I have read them but forget their meaning.

We Should Talk, *Bon Gérard*

For Gérard de Nerval

We should talk, *bon Gérard*.
We should sit at a café table at the bottom of a sandstone cliff
Beyond the tamarisk that infests the river bank.
We should drink new cider and ponder over the glyphs incised in the stone.
We should find arrowheads in the sand and lay them out on the table and speak of them.
We should make a sonnet of the glyphs.
We should inscribe the sonnet on an arrowhead
And drop it back onto the sand as we walk on into the October night.

Tactical Maneuver

fall in and commence the march down the river between the red sandstone cliffs, our feet always two inches above the water. Occasionally one of us steps out of formation to linger before a cliff and scratch a visual record of our march into the patina and must be called back to his duty before his attitude infects the entire platoon, for discipline, though it is not harsh, must be maintained, and loyalty is valued above all, even as we pass through the cottonwoods of a broad, flat bottom off the river, attentive to the encyphered chirpings of the birds and mindful of the traps beneath our feet, for here we must walk on the ground. (You may notice that we are avoiding parataxis insofar as possible.) We were told in the pre-operational briefing that it is suspected that some birds are scouts for the enemy that hides in a side canyon that we were assured we will recognize when we see it. The red birds, the ones that flit among us and pause suddenly without warning an inch before our faces, are the least trusted, but we are not permitted to harm them, for their disloyalty is not yet certain, and it is necessary to retain their goodwill. Back on the river (not precisely *on* the river; remember that we march two inches above it), a "Jodie" is heard rising from the rear, one voice at first, then two, and then it is picked up by the whole platoon. Even as we sing, we remain vigilant for traps built into the air through which we march, for the enemy is crafty, and I have seen, in these situations, three men at a time vanish, and either they are never seen again or their corpses are found days later, undeteriorated (autopsies indicating that they have died of asphyxiation only minutes before their corpses are discovered), but naked, their BDUs, which are always freshly laundered, being neatly folded and set on a nearby boulder with their boots atop them neatly laced. We talk of this when we sit in the shade of cottonwoods eating our meager rations, occasionally throwing a crumb to the red birds (the others never show any interest). Before we reach our destination, I myself step into a trap and find myself sitting alone, waiting, on a high four-legged stool in a complex latrine where all is white porcelain and the urinals and wash basins are built into steeply banked terraces and are difficult to distinguish one from the other and the water in the trough at the bottom of the opposite wall (it might be intended for urination but one cannot be sure) overflows, and I see that it will not be possible to keep water out of my shoes if I risk using it. I do not remember that this was mentioned in the briefing, but I might be mistaken, though I repeatedly review, as I wait, the whole presentation in my mind, endeavoring, insofar as possible, to avoid

I Find You at the Box End

I find you at the box end of a long, winding canyon. The sides are perpendicular and high, and there is no visible way out, the sides in fact rising so high that they converge in perspective above us. It has been hypothesized that if you could scale any of the three walls you would find that it is a Möbius strip that returns you to your starting point; but a steady stream of dreams issues from the end wall above my head, implying a source beyond the surface of the stone, and flows on back the way I have come. I do not find all of you in one place; you are scattered in parts embedded in the walls; but the parts are soft and warm, definitely flesh, and I am comforted by your presence around me as I feel about with my fingertips on the end wall, seeking the way through.

The Old Woman Who Carries a Basket on Her Back

The old woman who carries a basket on her back,
   she has walked far.
She has stories,
   and she will tell them.
Let her sit by the fire,
   let her sit on blankets,
      give her a piece of salmon.
Listen with respect,
   she will tell her stories;
      she will show what she carries in her basket.
She carries stones;
   the stones are words;
they are smoothed by water;
   they have rested on a river bottom a long time.

Do You Think God Wants to Withdraw His Ad?

Do you think God wants to withdraw his ad?
Do you think he cares a fig for precedent?
Squeeze an apple till the juice drips from it
See the visions in the drops
They flicker like a TV screen
See the lone figure in the distance
Approaching on an otherwise deserted shore
The water is choppy
It is nervous
The scene is printed on wallpaper
The surface of driftwood is soft
Make a groove in it with a thumbnail
Squeeze an apple till the juice drips from it
God cares nothing for precedent

God Is That Fat Woman in the Apron

God is that fat woman in the apron
Standing on the wet concrete floor of a fruit processing plant
Where a child pedals by on a gleaming red tricycle.
The fat woman is old, she has seen much, nothing surprises her.
She watches television at home in her apartment,
Sitting comfortably on a worn sofa,
Hoping for company,
Beer in her Frigidaire,
Cookies in her oven.

As We Sit Together in the Living Room of the Old House

As we sit together in the living room of the old house,
Waiting for someone to be first to speak,
The girl we all recognize arrives with a message.
Printed on white paper is what we do not speak
But all know.

Existenz

Eventually one sleeps and eliminates,
But little else seems quite necessary, although
The longing for sexual release becomes intense, but
Eat? One could simply not take the trouble;
One could take a fetal position and say,
"I would prefer not to";
But thirst is another matter,
And few would not recoil from fire.

The Sewing Machine Needle of Truth Floats Free

The sewing machine needle of truth floats free
This is a message written on the underside of leaves
The face peering through the foliage without expression
Painted with streaks black and white
Has been seen examining an assortment of sewing machine needles
The whole cluster of images rises from the depths of a lake
It hovers above streaming downward the letters of the Roman alphabet

Snowflakes Distance Themselves from the President

Snowflakes distance themselves from the president
He rides a red tricycle over the horizon
A series of explosions occurs nightly
But small animals pass on a trail through the grass in an endless
    stream
They are not impressed by clever moves on a checkers board
Nevertheless the game must proceed
Much depends on it
The pieces are enclosed in fur sewed tightly
Tight as the grip of a small hand on the handle of a salt mill
All floating into the night toward the center of the Milky Way

Squanto Steps on a Dry Twig

Squanto steps on a dry twig
The stones in every direction vibrate with the trauma
Even flies disintegrate in the shock wave
The coordinating committee meets on the steps of the Hôtel de Ville to discuss strategy
Squanto is late; the senior members are worried
The parking lot is hot and a dried snakeskin is caught in a door handle
And they know that every revolution devours its children
And Squanto disperses into the lines of a wiring schematic

Staring Down a Fish

Staring down a fish
Skeins of yellow silk billow up about us
Long ago we made a journey by train
The Logos billowing up from the smoke stack
Across the prairie sped the black locomotive
The Logos dispersing behind it, one vast herd of silver buffalo
Skeins of yellow silk billowing above them
Through the window of a passenger car staring down a fish

After the Next War

After the next war, white arms will grow up from the soil
They will undulate gently and futilely, raised toward the sky
After the next war, we will sit in dark rooms looking out through
 broken glass
We will recall the odor of cinnamon
We will see from the backs of our heads
After the next war, all the TV networks will show endless reruns of
 The Sound of Music
After the next war, ants will emerge endlessly from cracks in the
 walls
The birdbath in the flower garden will dream of becoming a
 sundial
Little girls will write imaginary words in imaginary alphabets on
 picture windows with white lipstick
We will see this through the cracks in the back of our heads
After the next war, the sidewalks will end
>> at the water's edge
>> in prepositions
>> at cliffs' edges
>> at the open doors of stripped Buicks
>> in premature ejaculations
>> at vacant lots where the ground is soft as
>>> decayed flesh under the feet
>> in midair at the abrupt ends of bridges
>>> over water far below
>> in the middle of sentences

After the next war I-5 through Seattle will be clogged by migrating
 deer

I-5 will remember working at Boeing
Julie Andrews will stand on a hilltop trying to hold together with
 both hands one breast that is a broken white dinner plate

Biographical Note

Colin Blaine Douglas was born in 1944 and brought up in Western Washington; is an enrolled member of the Samish Indian Nation; became a Latter-day Saint at the age of sixteen; served in the Brazilian Mission in 1964–1966; served in Military Intelligence in the Regular Army and the Utah National Guard, retiring as a sergeant first class; attended the University of Washington as a journalism major and received a bachelor's degree in psychology and a master's degree in American literature at Brigham Young University; was employed for twenty years as an editor in the Curriculum Department of The Church of Jesus Christ of Latter-day Saints; edited and reported for the *Magna* (Utah) *Times* newspaper for two years; with the former Linda Jean Wells, to whom he was married in 1969, is the father of seven; has resided in Utah since 1971; as literary favorites names Latter-day Saint scripture (including the Bible), Arthur Rimbaud, André Breton, Ezra Pound, T. S. Eliot, Kenneth Rexroth, Gary Snyder, and Philip Lamantia; is the author of *First Light, First Water; Glyphs;* and *Six Poems by Joseph Smith*.

www.ingramcontent.com/pod-product-compliance
Lightning Source LLC
LaVergne TN
LVHW041547070426
835507LV00011B/977